UNLEASHED: VISION 2020

© Copyright 2019 by Puissance Maison Publishing. All rights reserved.

ISBN 13: 978-0-9963661-5-1

This document is written towards providing quality and reliable information with regards to the topic and issues covered. The publication is sold with the idea that despite the contents of the document, the publisher is not rendering accounting, legal, medical, mental health advice, or any other professionally qualified services. If advice is necessary, legal or professional, a practiced individual in the profession should be consulted.

The information provided herein is stated to be truthful and consistent, in that any liability, in terms of inattention or otherwise, by any usage or abuse of any policies, processes, or directions contained within is the solitary and utter responsibility of the recipient reader. Under no circumstances will any legal responsibility or blame be held against the publisher for any reparation, damages, or monetary loss due to the information herein, either directly or indirectly.

Table of Contents

INTRODUCTION

"To the person who doesn't know where he wants to go, there's no favorable wind."-Seneca

Have you ever started to do something without even understanding why you're doing it or where you want to do it? Have you ever felt that you were knowledgeable about many things, but it seems like not enough?

How have you felt in such circumstances? Exhausted? Confused? Drained? Overwhelmed? Lost? Dissatisfied?

Have you ever thought about why you might feel tired, confused, drained, overwhelmed, lost or unhappy despite all the operational success that you've had?

The primary reason for many of these feelings is the absence of a **Vision** as a motivator!

Without vision, you're like a ship's captain whose compass doesn't work. Without vision, you're like a driver who doesn't know how to get to his destination. Without vision, you're like a traveler who doesn't understand where she's going or her trip's objectives.

Unfortunately, many organizations have no powerful vision, or if they do, they don't communicate their vision correctly. Either way they don't succeed in the long run, particularly in moments like economic crises.

Authentic leaders are visionaries in both their private and professional lives. They generate strong visions, transmit the vision to the individuals on their teams, and motivate the team to turn the leader's vision into a reality. Having a clear image of where we want to be or what we want to be is essential to staying on track to reach not only the right path to the destination, but also achieve the goal itself.

Vision demonstrates the image of the end result. Vision goes beyond even when the physical eyes can see. It's like you're playing with your imagination. A strong vision will assist you in getting a glimpse of the larger image. When you see the big picture, you can connect the dots and understand why some things happen.

With vision, you are no longer stuck in the details, worrying yourself about the minutia and minor local events happening here and there, especially during tough times. You don't count temporary setbacks as mistakes. By seeing the larger image, you know you need to face difficulties and adversities to get closer to achieving your vision. As a visionary leader, the unexpected storms are no longer surprising because you see the big picture, so you're always ready.

Vision Enables Concentration. Without a clear vision, short-term objectives may distract you. You may lose control of your boat as you hit unexpected storms. A strong vision enables you to concentrate on what is worthy of your time and attention and what will ultimately bring you to your destination. When you're concentrated, you're not scared of what's going on before you because with your vision compass, you turn the wheel of your boat towards your destination.

Vision Provides Direction. When you define a clear, powerful vision, you know where you're going. Your vision unfolds an invisible map highlighting where you need to go and how you need to get there. If you sail your boat in darkness without vision, the likelihood of getting lost is high because you have nothing to guide you. No compass, no stars, no map, nothing. When there's no destination, there's no direction.

Vision Inspires Motivation. An efficient vision can motivate your organization towards a common goal with a united front. While many may claim to have visions for their organizations, communities, or businesses, their visions may not be motivating enough to excite individuals in those organization to move towards that vision.

Vision Causes Stretching. A strong vision usually suffices to challenge the dreamer. It enables the leader and supporters to stretch and boost their abilities. The greater the capability of the team, the easier it is to accommodate change without negative impact. A good vision requires the leader to come from their comfort zone to accomplish what once seemed impossible.

Vision Energizes. Leaders' design and paint powerful and motivating visions. As mentioned above, passion turns on your beneficial energy generator switch. Therefore, your vision has the ability to maintain you in an energized state all the time. Your vision can fuel your journey by linking it to your enthusiasm and intent.

Vision is a Project Prerequisite. Without a great vision, great projects producing great results cannot be defined. That is, vision is a prerequisite for defining and prioritizing projects. If projects are not connected to vision, they may not succeed or may not serve any objective in the long run.

Action Without Vision. We can do a lot without vision but can accomplish a little. We may give up too quickly without vision. Developing a strong yet easy and clear vision for ourselves, our organization, and our individuals is essential.

WHAT IS A VISION?

Before we define vision, let's look at some vision interactions that are essential to its comprehension and implementation from an organizational, operational growth, and development perspective. Vision is best understood in terms of intent and mission. Purpose, vision and mission are like a three-stranded cord, when placed together, they enhance execution, strength, and exponentially increases the likelihood of success.

Purpose is the initial intention for something, the "why" in the mind of the creator or initiator. Vision is the inspiration that comes from intent, it is the "what" based completely on intent that comes from the creator's mind or initiator's mind. Mission is the particular systems and procedures used to achieve vision; it is the "how." Vision becomes effective through mission. Vision fulfills the purpose.

SO, WHAT'S VISION?

Vision is an Image of Intent. That part of intent, "the why," becomes noticeable enough to produce a crystallized image of "what. "Vision is your preferred future. It's the future you see as opposed to the present you're standing in.

Vision is Motivated by Truth. It's an image of reality through a prospective lens. As an adjective, potential is described as the ability to become or grow into something in the future. Potential is described as latent characteristics or skills that can be created, leading to future achievement or usefulness. Vision is straight linked to items that have yet to come out of you.

Vision With Intelligence. See your workplace through the lens of wisdom, knowledge, and comprehension. It also implies seeing your world through a lens that is beyond anything you presently know and comprehend. This becomes a catalyst that leads us beyond what we currently know and understand.

Vision is a key component in making any dream a reality. Vision is the capacity to see your dream or concept in the future. Until you are able to project yourself, 5, 10 years or more into the future, you will limit your ideas. Vision casting cannot be delegated to people who have no idea where the vision is coming from or going.

A vision must be futuristic-It speaks of what we see ourselves as a year, two or even 50 years from now. A vision has no focus on the past. It looks at what can be rather than focus on what has failed to happen.

Your vision must live beyond your time. Visions that exist only when the owner is available are not strong legacy visions. You must think generationally. Many years from now, your people should still be talking of your vision.

Your vision must be realistic, yet big. Sometimes people cast very large visions which others are scared to get involved in. Use your wisdom to ensure that though you may have a big vision inside, share it with people who support you. Share your vision with people who can help you think deeper and sharpen your approach to your vision.

You must be excited about your own vision. There is no need to pursue what you are not passionate about. If you are not passionate about your vision, then stop and rethink.

CHARACTERISTICS OF A VISION

What is vision? Is it something that only great leaders and great achievers have? If you have ever desired something that you don't have right now, and have imagined the picture of you having that, you've had a vision. If you have ever wanted to be a better version of yourself and have imagined yourself doing things in a better way, you've had a vision.

Vision is simply a visualization of something that you don't have right now. So, ask yourself, who do you want to be at the end of the year? What do you want to have? What do you want to accomplish? The ideas that you form right now to answer those questions are the beginnings of your vision for yourself by that particular time.

Vision is the starting point for success. If you desire success, but do not have a clear picture of what success looks like, then you are destined for a life of unfulfillment and frustration. This is simply because you will never know when you have reached your intended destination. So why is it that success eludes most people when having a vision is very much within their reach?

There are two possible reasons. One is that they do not know how to create an effective vision. Another is that they do not know how to bring their vision into reality. Let's address the first problem here.

So, what is an effective vision?

It is Achievable. This is what differentiates vision from a dream or a fantasy. An effective vision is one that you should be reasonably capable of realizing. This doesn't mean that you can achieve it without any effort on your part; it just means that it has to be something that is in line with the talents and resources currently accessible to you.

You'll want to challenge yourself, to grow and become a person with a bigger capacity for achieving. A great way to do this is to create a vision that makes it necessary for you to be stretched and expand your area of expertise.

It is Clear. You might have a vague picture of what you want to see in your life right now. A clear picture needs to be specific and it needs to be quantified. What does it look like? Can you describe it to someone else? Will that person see the same vision that you are seeing? That is the ultimate test of the clarity of your vision. Don't be afraid to put a concrete figure to your desires. By applying this criterion to your vision from the start, you will avoid a lot of wasted time and effort along the way.

Your vision must have a deadline. Don't be afraid to set it, and then to tell your accountability partner(s) about it. This will give you a tremendous sense of urgency which will motivate you to get it done. This criterion also forces you to stay focused on the most essential tasks when actioning your vision. Set your deadline for your vision today.

VISION BOARDS

2020 is upon us, and many have already discontinued their New Year resolutions. Whether it's weight loss or a promotion, everyone has objectives they want to accomplish. A vision or dream board can assist define and explain your objectives. A vision board is an easy method to assist you accomplish your objectives. Basically, the vision board addresses the second problem identified above, it shows how to bring the vision into reality.

A vision or dream board is a visual depiction or collage of things that you would like to complete in your life. It is a straightforward yet strong instrument that activates the law of attraction to start manifesting your dreams. The concept is that when you surround yourself with pictures of what you want from life, your life changes to suit those pictures and wishes.

The vision board idea has been around for centuries, but interest in the concept was renewed after talk show host and media mogul Oprah Winfrey acknowledged collecting photos and creating a vision board depicting Illinois Senator Barack Obama winning the presidential election.

A vision board is typically a big poster board with a collage of pictures, sketches and/or text on it. By choosing photos and phrases you're enthusiastic about, you'll start manifesting those things in your lives. Vision boards make your objectives visible and remind you of your objectives. You can choose how you visualize your future objectives in life.

Before creating your vision board, sit silently and ask yourself what you really want.

Building your vision board should be enjoyable. Indeed, it should be a pleasure! Building your vision board does not have to be accomplished all at once; it can be a gradual method. The concept, however, is to get started and move towards your dreams. Your objectives and dreams may alter with movement. It's okay to fine-tune your dreams as you travel towards them.

Your vision panel should represent who you want to be and what your workplace and surroundings will be. While many individuals cover their vision boards with images of material goods, providing room for personal development and a vision of who you want to be is essential. While material goods often bring great joy, they don't define you. While financial stability is important as a foundation, your goals should include where you will be after your foundation is built. Think of almost any famous multi-millionaire interviews. With few exceptions, they'll speak about who they are, what they're doing, their next project, and what's inspiring. Their money isn't who they are; they are their drive, goals, ambition, and vision.

Don't ignore non-financial objectives in your vision board. Set clear objectives of who you want to be, what you want to achieve, and include them in your vision board.

Integrate your vision into your everyday life. Refer to your vision board daily. Let the images and words help strengthen and shape your inner vision. Let your vision board help shape you and your environment. Work daily to become your mind's and board's vision! When faced with life situations, project choices, or decisions stop and consult your vision board. Does this activity or choice bring me nearer to my objectives? Is it in alignment with who I am and what I want to be?

WHY HAVE A VISION BOARD

Consider this, you start a weight loss journey motivated and pumped up. You've eaten clean and worked out for a week. But as soon as the second week begins, you land a huge deal and now you're focusing on the deal. Good for you, but what about weight loss?

Our brain is a beautiful thing! That which the mind can conceive, and you believe, you will achieve! But, as we regularly cope with so many facets of our life, staying focused and directing all your energy to one objective becomes incredibly hard.

Does that mean you can **only** concentrate on one goal at a time?

Absolutely not, our brain is wired to multitask. The only assistance we need is prioritization and motivation. You send the brain a signal to recognize, memorize, and implement your goals in the order of their importance to you.

That is the easy part. Motivation, however, is tricky ground. It's not hard to find your motivation; the hard part is to remain in that newfound motivation constantly. Your brain won't help you; it won't wake you up with a motivated mind every day, unless you help.

That's where the Vision Board comes in. A Vision Board is like a normal bulletin board filled with life goals, motivational pictures or texts, statements, planner, progress report, and anything else that helps keep your focus on the goal.

The basic attraction law principle is visualization and belief. The vision board serves a better objective, making visualization much easier.

Never lose focus. You have everything to stay on the track with a vision board. You don't have to make an effort to go through the why, what, and how. This helps you keep focused on the goal even if your attention manages to wander away from it for a while.

Seeing is much better than imagining. It's simple, if you have your goals before you, even if it's just written words on paper, it has a bigger impact. Your vision board is your personal glimpse of the future, how you feel, and what the situation would be like once you get there.

TYPES OF VISION BOARDS

There are several different kinds of vision boards. You may find that one of these boards is just the one for you:

•**Crystal Clear** - This board is used when you have a very clear vision of what you want for your future. Look for exact images and word sets. For instance: you're going to Paris within a year. You'll look for a picture that represents Paris (maybe the Eiffel Tower) and maybe the word or number 1, etc. Over the months, this board may not need editing because your objective is crystal-clear.

•**In flux** - This board is used when you're not sure what you want, or you're not sure where to go or what to do. You'll be searching for pictures and phrases that talk to you to fine-tune your direction. This board is edited much more than the Crystal Clear board.

•**Themed** - Use this board style if you're working on a given region of your life, or maybe it's your birthday or other event. You may want your birthday to manifest something specific. You could include your age and words that reflect what you want to achieve by your birthday, or what you want to make the event a success.

•**Categories** - Give careful consideration to several fields of your life that you may want your vision board to reflect either individually or as a whole: purpose or mission, service, finance, spiritual, faith, health, relationship, career, business, etc.

A vision board can operate because you can use it as a visual reminder and strengthen your ideas about your objectives and dreams.

CREATING A VISION BOARD

Vision boards are a strong method to use when making some inspirational and positive life changes. A vision board is all about you, what you want, do and have.

A vision board, also known as a dream board or treasure map, is merely a collection of pictures, words, quotes, or sentences that inspire you, or depict what you want. Our minds function in images, so you'll discover your motivation and inspiration last longer by getting a visual representation of what you're working towards and achieve your dreams much quicker.

Before creating your vision board, spend some time deciding precisely what you want. For everyone, this is completely different and there is no correct or incorrect goal. Take a look at the various arenas of your life including physical health, spirituality, career, finances, family, friendship, and mental health.

You can choose to build a vision board that includes everything you're working towards, or you may want to make several distinct boards for distinct focal points.

To make your vision board you'll need a few things such as: different kinds of magazines, a main surface such a poster board or a canvas, glue, scissors, and anything else you might want to use to decorate your board, including paint, glitter, stickers, ribbons etc. To get in the correct frame of mind and enable your spirituality and creativity to soar, attempt to create a calm and relaxed atmosphere. Things such as lighting a candle, putting on some relaxing music, or whatever works for you to bring you to a spiritual center. Now begin looking through your magazines for any images, words, quotes or sentences that inspire you, make you feel great, or seem to be connected to you.

Don't worry if you're pulling photos that don't seem to be linked to your objectives or intent. Allow yourself to take as many pictures as you like. Just have fun and cut out photos, words, quotes or sentences that appeal to you.

When you have a wonderful stack of cut-outs sitting beside you, begin looking at what you have. You might like to sort them into stacks, e.g. career, family, health, inspiring quotes, etc. Notice if there's one pile larger than the others.

Look through each stack and pick the photos you want on your vision board. Choose the photos, words, quotes and sentences that stir the most emotion in you because that's what will re-ignite your inspiration as you concentrate on your vision board.

You can begin putting them on your poster board once you've chosen what you want. Once you're pleased with the design, you can position them. Please complete your layout before you start gluing your pictures down, as you don't want to destroy any of your images by attempting to remove them once you've glued them.

You can decorate your board. You may want to write inspirational words on your board. You may want to add some paint, glitter, stickers or ribbon or just leave it as it is. This is your vision board, and you create it just as you like.

Finally, hang your Vision Board. The best place to hang your vision board is somewhere you see it regularly. Bathroom or your walk-in closet, refrigerator, etc. It does not matter where you put it, as long as you see it all the time. The more you see your vision board, the more your subconscious sees what you really want, and the more your subconscious hears and sees what you want, the quicker you get outcomes.

HAVING SUCCESS WITH A VISION BOARD

Use It- Looking at the board will make you always conscious of your dreams and objectives.

Believe It - Remember, much of your vision board achievement is thinking you deserve what your board reflects. This faith will be the catalyst for you to do what's essential to attain your objectives and dreams.

Update It - As your vision and dreams change, remember to update your vision board. You want what you've imagined moving consistently into the concrete globe.

Continue to use your vision board to assist you to clarify and concentrate your objectives and dreams. Just because you put an image on your board that doesn't manifest in your life within 2 months doesn't mean it doesn't function. You must stay patient, use the tool, believe you deserve what you've imagined and live your life. It will happen if you maintain faith and let the Universe materialize results that seem like miracles.

There are Online methods to generate a virtual board. You can also load apps to your computer and have your vision board right on your desktop if you prefer that path.

Whatever format you use, a vision board is one of the strongest ways to transform your mindset and life!

HOW TO MANIFEST A VISION BOARD

How was your last year or your year so far? Are you attracting what you want? Are you on track to achieve the objectives you're working towards? How do you feel about yourself and overall life?

Now is the time to look at YOUR Vision Board and get to "KNOW THYSELF." Throughout my life, my mentors have advised me to "understand myself." Why? Because I am stronger than I think.

We continually attract our reality to us, and our reticular activating systems (the portion of our brains that operates like a spam filter) always filter out any power, situation or individual that does not suit our inner world representation.

That's one of many reasons to create a Vision Board, a visual representation of the objectives and dreams you want to express. The visual element of your objectives, your end results, will program your subconscious mind and use your reticular activating scheme as a guide to give you the truth you want.

Looking at your board today, do you still feel empowered, excited, like you could just step directly into the truth you observe?

If you reply yes, fantastic! Enjoy your vision board and practice your visualizations and affirmations. Eventually you will discover that your vision and your reality will synchronize and you will be in the correct location at the correct moment. You will receive fresh thoughts, intuitive nudges, and "flashes of inspiration" that will guide you to the correct steps toward your visions and enable the law of appeal to give you your dreams.

On the other hand, when you look at your vision board, do you get any impressions of anxiety, pain, a twinkling of regret, any unpleasant thought, weight on your shoulders, or a sinking sensation in your belly.

Remove the image or images that are causing those types of reactions within you!

This method is powerful! Having a vision board in complete perspective programs your conscious and unconscious minds, but if the images no longer resonate well for you, it's much easier to get them "out of sight!" You should do this because if those images are causing uncomfortable emotions, you will counteract the manifestation power.

VISION BOARD DON'TS

Anyone can cut and paste photos on a board, but few individuals know what to do to realize their dreams and objectives that they have selected to put on their vision boards. Even fewer individuals understand when they are "off-track".

Below are the top things to avoid when manifesting your dreams and objectives using a visual device like a vision board.

Believe that it will not happen.

One of the first things to ask yourself is, "Is this really feasible? Do I deserve it?" To attract and manifest your dreams, you must believe that it can occur for you. You must have that profound internal knowledge to accomplish and embrace that objective. You must believe it, it's not just IF, but WHEN?

Take no action.

For some, their vision board will sit on the wall, the mirror, the fridge or even be hidden in a closet. About 5 percent of people, just because they've created their board, a visual manifestation of their written goals and dreams, it'll be enough and their goals will materialize, like magic! It has a logical explanation, but its more enjoyable to think of it as magic! We're going to have to do something to assist the vision board's function for us. Some will do a regular visualization exercise; others will create a strategic action plan. There are many personal development methods you can use to accelerate your dreams. Doing a daily exercise is the key, creating a creative pattern that promotes you on your path toward achievement.

Hearing negativity.

Beguiling attitudes. People have the ability to influence others, and there's an old saying, "Birds of a feather flock together." So, if you can't surround yourself with upbeat, positive-focused people, make sure you protect yourself from rampant negativity.

Expect it all to go "effortlessly."

This is the cause of many broken dreams and new-year resolutions. When the going gets tough and you do not understand that to achieve a dream or goal, there may be some learning or stumbling blocks along the way. Be open to difficulties and some increasing discomforts. It will be worth achieving your dreams.

Do it for someone else.

This is enormous in our culture. So many individuals give up on their dreams and compromise to please others. You have a journey, a reason to be here. Discover who you are and build what you really want. Create your vision board and make sure you look at it every day!

EXECUTING YOUR VISION

Then the LORD replied: "Write down the revelation and make it plain on tablets so that a herald may run with it."
Habakkuk 2:2

Think of the individuals who produced exceptional companies from the ground up; individuals who have accomplished exceptional achievement such as Bill Gates, Tyler Perry, & Oprah Winfrey to name a few. What did they need to understand their vision?

They were prepared to take risks by activating their faith. They never stopped pursuing their vision. Some individuals have a powerful vision of themselves and their lives. For some, it comes naturally. Others, not so much. We may have some vague thoughts, wishes and hopes, but a vision? Usually not.

How do you generate and understand your vision? Well, you've got to think. It's exploring. Exploring you and what's crucial to you. It's an exercise, it requires some work. But once you spend time, you're on the path to an exceptional existence with liberation, energy, and prosperity.

"Big thinking precedes an excellent accomplishment". (Wilferd Peterson) How large can you imagine? When developing your perspective, ask yourself the questions that make you think of your larger than life image. What legacy are you leaving behind? These questions can be hard to answer, requiring a journey of self-discovery to determine what really matters to you.

Ask yourself questions such as:

- What life do you want?
- What is it going to take for you to accomplish that?
- What difference would it create for you, your family, your society, and the world?

"Long-term people hit only what they want."-Henry David Thoreau

You must be prepared to let go, say goodbye to convictions that may prevent you from articulating and pursuing your vision. Release your beliefs that tell you, "I don't have time to think about the future," or "I need to deal with the problems of today." Your beliefs can limit you, telling you that you can't accomplish your dreams or visions. Don't let your convictions prevent you from completely exploring your vision. Don't deny exploration because you can't get there. Today's ideas generate your future. Be prepared to see what that sight is, despite what you think may occur.

Picture your sight. Imagine being successful and achieved. Imagine sights, colors, odors, sounds, tastes, feelings. Now, imagine your life if your vision was achieved.

More questions to ask yourself as you create your vision:

- What's your definition of success?
- What does an exceptional life mean to you?
- What kind of person would you have to accomplish your vision?

Write down your vision. You must describe, imagine, believe. Be prepared to think large, larger than you believe. Vision is beyond sensible and predictable. Write about relationships, home, career advancement, events, etc. The more detail you write down, the more genuine it becomes.

Create your vision daily. Commit to create your future now. You create your vision with your ideas. Practice building your vision every day. Be your current vision fulfillment. Bring it in now. You don't get your vision by waiting for it. You must set goals to the items on your vision board.

The only way to predict the future is to have the authority to shape it. Sharing your vision with others makes it more real for you. When you talk, you become it. You won't look like a fool, you will be in action. The more you tell individuals what you expect, the more prepared you are to take action to produce outcomes.

Taking action is the most significant piece. You must act to fulfill your vision. You take action to ensure achievement. You look at the future, with belief in your vision, and you do the steps to get what you see for yourself. Your vision won't come true only through thinking. You must take action to meet your vision. You must take actions consistent with the life you see. You must never stop or give up!

CONCLUSION

What vision have you spent years discussing, but never fulfilled? You may have lost precious time saying, "One day I'll begin my own company, next month I'll begin a savings plan, or next year I'll return to college." Seven years and a pile of bills later, you're still saying the same. You are still stuck singing the same ancient song.

Evaluate your location. See how your life lines up in the seven fields of life (spiritual, relational, physical, mental, economic, social and professional). Knowing where you are, you will be able to see what you need to do to get where you want to be. If you need to make improvements now, then do it **now** and don't wait for tomorrow.

Make sure what you're planning aligns with what you're vision is, not what someone else has planned for your life. Set a definite plan. Create a clear private vision statement documenting where you want to go. It should obviously define what you want most in life, how you will get there, and a timeline to make your vision is a reality.

You must remove distractions immediately because discouraging conversation and behavior can cause you to forfeit your vision. Explore your options. Look at it from a wide-open lens. Focus on your vision but maintain your peripheral sight open to all accessible alternatives.

Enlist accountability partners. You'll need some help, but only enlist those willing to encourage and walk with you even when they can't see it, and things don't make sense.

Execute your vision. Having a documented plan, it's time to take action. Do not waste time worrying about what others will say or how things will work, just begin implementing your plan. What good is a well-written vision plan, if you never take action?

Examine the process. As you take action on your vision, you will need to monitor your process continuously to see where you are on the right path. Examining your vision method frequently will tell you if you need any adjustments or modifications.

VISION BOARD AFFIRMATIONS

As you are developing your vision board, you should consider adding affirmations to it to help change your mind set in the year ahead! Speak the affirmations on your board out loud, and into your life on a daily basis. Below are some examples of affirmations that you can use:

- My self-confidence is growing stronger every day

- I am free of limiting beliefs and open to limitless possibilities

- I am enjoying all the benefits of eating mindfully

- Every day I feel healthier, happier, and more energetic

- I am open to receiving all the abundance the universe is offering me

- I am debt free and grateful for all the money that is flowing into my life

- I am focused on my goals and enjoying my career

- I am surrounded by co-workers who are positive, enthusiastic, and supportive

- I love myself and this new life that I have created

- I always remain calm and peaceful, even in the midst of chaos

- I am living my dream life

- I choose hope over fear

- Positivity is a choice that I choose to make

- I will not take other people's negativity personally

- I will stop apologizing for being myself

- Negative self-talk has no place in my life

- I do not bow to my fears

- My mind, body, and soul are fit and strong

- I am committed to becoming the person God wants me to be

- Success is in my future

- I am here for a reason and it is clear to me now

www.ingramcontent.com/pod-product-compliance
Lightning Source LLC
Chambersburg PA
CBHW021122020426
42331CB00004B/587